Gardening WITH THE EXPERTS

ORGANIC

Gardening WITH THE EXPERTS

ORGANIC

MOIRA RYAN

HARLAXTON
PUBLISHING

Photographs: Douglass Baglin Photography courtesy Weldon Trannies: opposite title page, pages 6, 22.
Bay Picture Library: pages 20, 28, 31, 36, 37, 38 (above left), 39 (above), 42 (right).
M. Darlington courtesy Weldon Trannies: page 35.
Ray Joyce courtesy Weldon Trannies: page 8 (below).
The Garden Picture Library: Michael Howes 13, Brian Carter 18, Ron Sutherland 39 (below).
Mary Moody: pages 7, 8,(above), 10, 11, 14-15, 16, 19 (right), 21 (above), 23, 24, 25, 26, 27,
30, 32, 33, 34, 38 (above right), 40 (below), 41, 42 (left), 44-45.
Tony Ryan: pages 19 (left), 21 (below), 29, 38 (below), 40 (above).
Weldon Trannies: front cover, page 12.

Published by Harlaxton Publishing Ltd
2 Avenue Road, Grantham, Lincolnshire, NG31 6TA, United Kingdom.
A Member of the Weldon International Group of Companies.

First published in 1990 (Limp)
Reprint 1991 (Cased)
Reprint 1992 (Cased)
Reprinted 1993

Publishing Manager: Robin Burgess
Illustrations: Kathie Baxter Smith
Typeset in UK by Seller's, Grantham
Produced in Singapore by Imago

British Library Cataloguing-in-Publication data.
A catalogue record for this book is available from the British Library.
Title: Gardening with the Experts: Organic.
ISBN:1 85837 028 0

Contents

THE HEALTHY GARDEN

Modern, commercial crop production, mines the soil for a quick return, using large quantities of artificial fertilisers and ignores the vital role of organic matter to maintain fertility. Varieties bred mainly for yield often have little disease resistance, so regular spraying is essential. This is expensive, potentially a form of environmental pollution and may leave trace residues in the produce. As organic matter in the soil is reduced (or even deliberately destroyed by burning to clear land), chemical fertilisers become less effective until the soil cannot produce a profitable crop, since organisms that make nutrients available to plants are no longer present.

There is concern that low soil fertility provides nutritionally poor produce and an increasingly poisoned environment, that will lead to a growth in malnutrition,

Above: An organic vegetable garden.
Page opposite: Vigorous growth in an ornamental garden.

Vine crops and corn, organically grown.

A home gardener at work.

disease and allergies as a direct result of vitamin and mineral deficiencies. Forward-looking, practical people working in the fields of agriculture and horticulture have realised that a different approach is vital. As they learn to work with nature, their findings are that it is possible to achieve good, sustainable yields of first-class, high quality produce.

Organic gardening is the ideal solution for home gardeners. Not only is there a health advantage by reducing the amount of chemicals in your environment, but also, organic materials involve a large degree of recycling, which tends to be a good deal cheaper than chemical sprays or fertilisers. Properly nourished plants, free of chemical stress suffer less from pests and diseases.

A balanced diet, rich in minerals, makes organically grown fruits and vegetables both health-giving and delicious. In an ornamental garden vigorous growth can be expected, with healthy foliage and flowers of particular brilliance. A well-organised organic garden is labour-saving, needs less spraying, digging, weeding or watering.

THE SOIL

Minerals in undisturbed virgin or grassland soils are replenished by rock disintegration while organic matter is supplied by rotting vegetation. With the addition of animal droppings and corpses of animals that feed off the plants, a recycling system is formed. Some natural soils lack certain minerals. This affects the type of plants they support as well as the health of animals.

The aim of organic gardening is to set up a recycling system under cultivation, to rectify any deficiencies.

SOIL TYPES

Soil character depends on the content of organic matter coupled with the chemical composition and texture.

Sand has the largest particles separated by spaces through which water can drain rapidly. They lack stability, organic matter

Above: Organic matter can be added in the form of compost.
Page opposite: Organic growing aims to set up a recycling system under cultivation.

Soil types range from sands to clays.

and many minerals. In contrast, clays have minute particles clinging closely together so that air and water penetrate them with difficulty, this makes them sticky when wet and concrete-hard when dry. Because it is mineral rich, clay can be broken down to fertile soils. Loams fall between these two extremes, with an average texture and amounts of nutrients. Light soils are useful for food production in cold regions since they warm rapidly in spring, while heavy clay-loams are best for retaining water in dry conditions.

A rough assessment of soil type can be made by moulding some moist soil in your hand. Light soils will feel gritty, and very sandy types will not form a ball. Medium soils ball without feeling gritty or sticky. Heavy loams feel sticky but do not become shiny when rubbed between the fingers. Soil that forms a firm shiny ball indicates clay-loam while if it forms an unyielding

solid ball, indicates clay.

Soils in the middle range will not need alteration and remain in good condition indefinitely if regularly topped up with organic matter. Very sandy soils need all the organic matter they can get to improve both fertility and water-holding capacity. Soils that shine when rubbed between the fingers need extra attention.

Mere digging never improves clay soils. The particles must be made to flocculate (form clumps), creating spaces for air and water. Spread 1 kg of gypsum (calcium sulphate) per square metre and work it into the top 6 cm of soil. After a few days apply a second dressing, forking over to a depth of 15 cm. Allow the soil to stand for some weeks and then, with it just slightly moist, work plenty of compost and some sand into the top 15 cm. Surrounding the fluffed-up soil with boards or blocks will allow continuing good drainage.

SOIL pH

Lime will improve clays, but it alters their pH, which is not necessarily desirable. The pH scale measures acidity.

A pH of 7 is neutral, readings above this are alkaline, and below are acid. A normal soil range is approximately 4.5 (virgin soil) to 1.5 (soils on limestone or chalk).

The pH level affects chemical solubility. Major plant nutrients (needed in large quantities) are at their most soluble around neutral and dissolve very little at 4.5.

Most trace elements (equally important, but needed in minute quantities) dissolve best in moderately acid conditions.

At 6.5 everything is reasonably soluble,

Page opposite: Preparing the soil for planting.
Pages overleaf: This vegetable patch has been built up and surrounded by boards to improve drainage.

Lettuces prefer a pH level of 7, while tomatoes do best with a level below 5.6.

but a great many plants grow successfully in any normal soil, from slightly acid to mildly alkaline.

Some plants prefer a special pH, notably *rhododendrons*, *proteas* and *heathers* which have a high iron requirement, so they will turn yellow if the soil is above a pH of 5. Above 6.5 many shade-loving plants behave similarly. While vegetables grow adequately at 6.5, onions, legumes, leafy vegetables, beets and rhubarb all prefer 7 or slightly higher, while tomatoes, potatoes and peppers are happiest below 5.6.

Soils can be sweetened by adding lime or dolomite and can be acidified with sulphur. Except in limestone areas, lime is often needed in new gardens. A home test kit gives a rough approximation, but it is safer to consult a test laboratory as overliming seriously affects growth. Once the pH is correctly adjusted, most soils that are given an adequate compost programme will need little further lime.

MAINTAINING FERTILITY

Organic gardeners maintain fertility by combining home-produced and other waste materials in the form of compost or mulch. Suitable domestic materials include lawn clippings, weeds, pruning waste, fallen leaves or flowers, spoilt fruit or vegetables, animal manure, food scraps, sweepings, paper, cotton, woollen stuffing and textiles (including carpets and underfelt). These can be supplemented with rock dust, industrial residues (for example, untreated sawdust, bark, mushroom compost, feathers and hair), straw, hay, pine needles and many other materials.

COMPOSTS

Composting will speed up recycling. The process begins with a high-temperature

bacteria needing oxygen, moisture and a suitable carbon/nitrogen ratio. The heat generated within the heap destroys most weed seeds and disease organisms.

For a big volume of material a simple compost heap is adequate, but less than 2 cubic metres needs a bin. Several types are satisfactory, provided they have sufficient ventilation and a protective cover. Wooden bins are usually available in sets of three, should be made from treated timber for long life. Chicken wire on a frame, or self supporting weldmesh, can be lined with cardboard or plastic pierced with holes which will avoid dry outer layers. Plastic bins are long-lasting and neat. A simple compost tumbler consists of a hand-rotated drum mounted on a frame.

Turning and mixing speeds up the compost process. In a daily rotated tumbler breakdown takes two weeks, while a totally unturned heap may take up to nine months. Heaps may be taken apart and rebuilt and material in wooden bins can be turned from one to another. Plastic or wire bins may be lifted off the heap and then the compost tossed back.

Breakdown is fastest when there is a ratio of approximately thirty times as much carbon as nitrogen. Carbon predominates in woody and mature materials such as

sawdust, autumn leaves, paper and straw. Animal wastes and lush foliage are high in nitrogen. Too little nitrogen produces a cold, slow breakdown, while excess results in a smelly process which wastes a lot of ammonia. Animal manure is not essential where other nitrogen is available, but it is valuable for supplying trace elements, as is seaweed. Dung from most farmyard animals is fairly low in nitrogen and can be used without composting. Pure chicken manure, dog droppings and especially pigeon manure contain a lot of nitrogen and are safer if composted as they may burn roots.

Preferably fill bins in one operation that mixes the ingredients or place alternate carbon- and nitrogen-rich layers. The base of the compost should have soil contact to

Add chicken manure to compost heaps.

attract organisms. More bacteria will be supplied by animal manure and the soil on weed roots. Where weeds are not included, small amounts of soil or manure should be mixed in. Sprinklings of gypsum will give the organisms the required calcium, but do not add lime. Waxy leaves, some woody residues and poor grass may not rot due to of lack of phosphorus, which can be added by chicken manure or *light* sprinklings of bone dust or bone flour. Thick stems rot poorly, so crush, chop or shred them, or pass them under a rotary mower. The base layer should be coarse, twiggy material for good aeration. Aeration can be improved by placing a central perforated plastic pipe or a roll of chicken wire as a chimney. Make sure all compost materials are moist, but not soaking wet. Cover them with a piece of plastic or old carpet.

If the compost heat does not give off a vigorous heat, check the levels of air and moisture and if necessary increase nitrogen. Turning a hot heap to mix in outer layers encourages even processing. When the heat dies away the material may be used at once or left until broken down completely to fine black humus.

Above: A weldmesh compost bins with plastic liners.
Page opposite: Lime and compost are often needed in new gardens.

First-stage compost is suitable for top-dressing.

First-stage compost is suitable for top-dressing established plants, and as humus for mixing into soil for new plantings.

Use compost sheet on spare plots in between rows of the vegetable patch or between plants in shrubberies. Slash down any crop residues, weeds or green manure crops. (Green manure crops are plants grown solely for the purpose of increasing organic matter in the soil.) Cover them with newspaper, about ten sheets thick and generously overlapped. Water the surface thoroughly then spread with grass clippings either alone or mixed with shredded wood or sawdust. (This will keep areas weed-free for three to six months.)

Compost made from a fertile garden is a complete plant food, if it is used generously most plants will flourish without additional chemical feeding.

MULCHES

These are covers for the ground that retain moisture, suppress weeds and control temperature extremes. Eventually they rot down and feed the soil. They may be made from any weed free organic material, but preferably from one that is slow-rotting. Before applying mulches, always remove any perennial weeds and water thoroughly.

Bark is best for ornamental beds, closely followed by home-shredded wood. Most

Bark chips used as mulch.

A large heap of leaf mulch.

weeds will be suppressed by a covering of 4cm of mulch or economise by using an underlay of newspaper. Untreated sawdust is suitable but sometimes robs the soil of nitrogen, then blood and bone should be scattered beneath it. Sawdust will pack down and may shed water if not stirred occasionally. Straw can be used on less windy sites. Half decayed autumnal leaves will be topped up annually but provide more food for plants than other mulches. Peat is expensive and tends to blow away when it has dried out. It is more useful in potting mixtures and planting composts for acid lovers.

Sheet composting with paper mulch.
The paper is covered with grass clippings.

PLANT STRESS

Plants suffer stress from excessive dryness or wetness, from wind and from unsuitable temperatures or light levels.

DRY AND WET CONDITIONS

There are various measures will help plants cope with dry, hot weather. In our ever changing world, the availability of water is an increasing and often expensive problem. Plan your garden so that plants which enjoy heat are exposed to the sun and reserve shady areas for plants that need cooler conditions.

Drought survival largely depends on deep rooting. There is a limit to what roots can penetrate. Natural hardpan and rock near the soil's surface are the main barriers for roots, but even compacting caused by earth-moving machinery can block their downward spread. Hard layers will impede

Above: Hand-watering the vegetable garden.
Page opposite: Successful gardens are the result of careful planning.

drainage so that roots often drown in wet weather. Root damage then makes plants vulnerable to drought. The first sign of distress occurs when soft tip growth droops and dies. Quick and copious watering will sometimes saves these plants.

Watering the garden generously at five or seven day intervals is better than daily light sprinkling. Effective watering depends on slow and thorough absorption. Drying of surface layers between watering helps soil aeration. New plants, especially shrubs and trees, need regular supplies of water.

Summer watering may be unnecessary for deep-rooted, mature plants if they are in a loose soil with plenty of organic matter and mulch, but watch for drooping tip growth. Use organic mulches, rocks or spreading ground covers to keep the ground cool and reduce evaporation. While most Northern Hemisphere plants need summer moisture, some southern shrubs (including many

Proteaceae) adapt to heat and drought with root dormancy. Watering these plants in late summer may start fatal root-rots.

Shallow growers like *rhododendrons, camellias* and citrus trees produce a wide spreading web of roots just below the soil's surface, protected in nature by a mulch of fallen leaves. Although some of these plants prefer to grow in part-shade, many will tolerate sun if the roots are in thickly mulched, humus-rich, moist soil.

Mulching and regular watering are essential in the vegetable garden. Most vegetables prefer sunny conditions but only grow copiously with a regular supply of moisture. New plants will often become established more easily if shielded for a few days with a shade cloth or leafy twigs.

Excessive rain, water run off and flooding is harder to cope with than drought.

In heavy soils the water table may come up close to the soil's surface during winter.

Regular watering is easy with a sprinkler system.

Mulching is essential in the vegetable garden.

Raised flower beds solve drainage problems.

SOLID BARRIERS CREATE DESTRUCTIVE TURBULENCE

STAGGERED WINDBREAKS SLOW AND DEFLECT WINDS

Thirty hours of submergence is about the limit for roots, even dormant ones. Bog or swamp plants may be used in small wet patches, but where a large part of garden is affected drains and possibly raised beds will be needed.

WIND

Providing shelter from winds needs careful planning. Solid objects give poor protection. There is always a small wind shadow behind a building, a solid wall or fence, or a thick hedge, but this is only because the wind has been forced up and over barriers; a little further out from it, the wind swoops down in a destructive swirl. Wind also blows around the sides of buildings, while a gap between two buildings, or even between dense trees, can act as a funnel.

Better protection comes from slowing the wind flow down. Using slatted fences,

A row of taller crops shelters the more delicate plants from the wind.

pierced walls, trees or shrubs with rather open growth, or open-weave plastic are all effective. Two or more plant species with different growth habits in staggered rows are often more effective than a single row of one kind. The higher the barrier, the larger the area that is protected. However, in many gardens sunshine and prevailing wind come from the same quarter so wind protection must be balanced against shade.

Most vegetables need sun but do poorly on windy sites. Not only will foliage be damaged, but crops that need warmth may produce nothing, because low temperatures prevent flowering, while pest and disease resistance may be reduced.

In those areas that cannot be protected use wind-tolerant species. There is an enormous variation in the amount of wind plants can stand. The softer the foliage, the more shelter is needed.

Coastal plants are a first choice, though some, being less hardy, may not be able to stand the severity of inland frosts.

Well-grown trees and shrubs normally remain upright and firmly anchored in anything short of a hurricane, but where roots cannot penetrate deeply nor develop

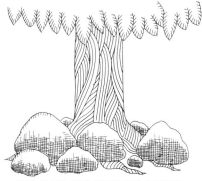

ROCKS PLACED OVER ROOTS GIVE SUPPORT

their full strength their hold is weakened. Trees on river banks may keel over due to a high water table.

Staking is essential for floppy growing plants like broad beans but should be used with caution on woody plants as it actually discourages strong root development. It is essential for newly planted trees, especially where roots have been severely cut back, but should be used for the shortest possible time. Encourage roots to become strong by allowing the tree to sway slightly.

Occasionally the wind breaks some prop roots on a mature tree. These are rarely replaced and rocking may cause all sorts of problems. Fasten such cripples permanently between a pair of stakes. Wind rock affects bulky shrubs, especially roses, forming a funnel in the soil at the base of the plant. Rain runs off into the funnel, saturates the root stock and leads to basal rot. If this is apparent attach the stem to a short stake and fill in the hole.

Permanent rocks left in place over root systems are better than staking for weak-rooted shrubs. Standard trained plants will need stakes tall enough to support the head, which may otherwise snap in wind. Loose elastic material ties should be looped around the stem and inspected regularly to avoid ringbarking.

TEMPERATURES

Heat can be tempered by shade and water, but cold weather is more of a problem. In frost-prone areas tender plants need to be moved into a winter shelter or provided with in situ cover. Many plants will survive light frosts if planted under house eaves or if covered on cold nights with plastic or even newspapers. Surround tender trees or shrubs with a light frame over which a cover can be thrown when frost threatens.

In very cold gardens it may be necessary to protect border plants with a mulch of bracken, sawdust or fallen leaves.

Some parts of gardens are particularly warm or cold. Use the warmest for half-hardy plants. The coldest sites will be low-lying where frost collects. Frost flows like water and settles in hollows, or ponds up where the downhill air flow is obstructed by a house or other solid barrier. These areas should be avoided when siting fruit trees, especially the early-flowering stone fruits, or crops may regularly fail to set.

Frost is an advantage for some hardy temperate crops, sweetening vegetables and stimulating fruit-bud formation. It reduces carry-over of many pests and diseases.

Above: One way of staking a newly planted tree.
Page opposite: Staking is necessary for floppy plants like peas.

29

Standard roses are supported by stakes.

In warm regions, Peach trees should be planted in the warmest parts of the garden.

LIGHT LEVELS

Plants adapt to different levels of light. Excessive sunshine will cause hard, yellow or highly coloured growth and sometimes with dead, whitish patches of sunburn.

Plants that are too heavily shaded grow spindly, with very dark, thin leaves and reduced flowering, while coloured foliage frequently reverts to a dull green.

In cold areas, citrus trees such as grapefruit should be covered when frost threatens.

HEALTH PROBLEMS

NUTRITION

A diet imbalance makes plants unhealthy. There are many essential nutrients and some (stored though not used) vital for the health of the animals that eat them, such as cobalt and selenium. Health problems are rare in plants fed on compost and organic manures and fertilisers.

The major nutrients needed in large amounts are:

NITROGEN

This element is important for growth, but an excess suppresses the uptake of potassium and phosphorus. Shoots become soft, attractive to pests and actually poisonous to mammals. Natural fixation of nitrogen from the air by bacteria in soil and legume roots occurs less in cold weather, causing weak, pale or bluish growth which responds to applications of dried blood.

Keep plants healthy with compost and organic manures and fertilisers.

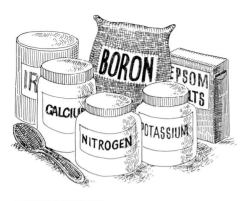

flowering and dull green or purple foliage. Corn leaves show purple stripes.

Seeds contain very little phosphorus, so adequate supplies are important when raising seeds. Bone dust and bone flour are the best organic sources, but the phosphorus takes time to become available so they are best applied in autumn. Bird manure contains plenty of phosphorus and if it is included in compost then deficiencies are highly unlikely.

PHOSPHORUS

Phosphorus is important for bulbs, grasses (including sweet corn) and generally for good root growth and fruiting, but *proteas* need very little.

A severe deficiency causes stunting of roots and shoots, the suppression of

POTASSIUM

This is needed for balanced growth and disease resistance. All potassium salts are soluble and quickly wash out of sands, but clay particles cling onto them. Apparent shortages may occur with excesses of both nitrogen and phosphorus. A deficiency causes browning of leaf margins, especially

Corn needs plenty of phosphorus from the soil.

A potassium deficiency causes an increase in chocolate spot fungus on beans.

ground limestone and dolomite. Dolomite has the same effect on pH as limestone, but also supplies magnesium.

MAGNESIUM

This is essential for *chlorophyll* formation. Deficient foliage may be yellow, but often the veins remain green on yellow or brown leaves. Deficiencies can be caused by an excess of either potassium or calcium, as well as scanty humus. For quick relief use Epsom salts at a rate of 30 gm/square metre dissolved in water, though for long-term correction use dolomite.

Shortages of trace elements are rare where compost is used regularly and is supplemented by animal manure, seaweed and especially seaweed extracts.

BORON

Some soils are completely lacking in boron, and a deficiency can be induced in others on gooseberries and many vegetables, blotchy ripening in tomatoes and increased chocolate spot fungus on beans.

Potatoes and tomatoes need a plenty of potassium. Wood ash contains potassium, so long as it has not been leached out by rain, but it is also high in lime. Russian comfrey and barley are other good sources.

CALCIUM

Calcium affects water balance but it is suppressed by excess potassium. A lack of calcium causes the death of growing points (the tissue at the tip of shoots, from which new growth arises), and with lack of water at critical periods, it contributes to blossom end rot on tomato and bitter pit in some young apples.

Potatoes show pale, stunted growth and minute tubers. Sources are wood ash,

Apple trees need sufficient boron.

Healthy plants are rarely affected by pests and diseases.

by heavy liming. This causes crown canker and root rot in beets, brown heart in turnips, brown curd in cauliflowers, corky spots on tomatoes and corky cracking of some apples and pears.

A shortage can be corrected with 15 gm of borax dissolved in 9 litres of warm water, applied over 6 square metres or sprayed on fruit tree foliage in late autumn.

IRON

Iron may not be absorbed by plants in soils where the pH is high from too much lime or from underlying limestone. Iron deficiencies affect mainly acid-loving shrubs, yellowing their foliage. A solution of chelated iron in water will be taken up even under alkaline conditions, or the soil may be acidified with sulphur.

PESTS AND DISEASES

Healthy plants have few problems with pests and diseases. Those affected are best dealt with by an integrated pest control that involves a minimal disruption to the environment.

1. Where possible, time planting to avoid periods with high risk of attack from pests or diseases.
2. Monitor plants closely without protective spraying. Anticipate attacks, then cover crops or set early-warning traps.
3. Remove infected leaves or shoots and pick or wash off pests. Foliage damage on fruiting plants around harvest time may be ignored.
4. Destroy all infected or infested crop residues.
5. Encourage predators of pests by keeping

Use biodegradable insecticides for unavoidable spraying.

spraying to a minimum and providing shelter and food.

6. For unavoidable spraying, use low risk biodegradable preparations. Many insecticides also destroy predators and pollinators, so wherever possible use narrow spectrum products or spray when desirable insects are not around. Some alternative sprays have been made from very dilute solutions of vitamised insect pests, and although their development is still at the experimental stage, these insecticides have proved very effective.

PESTS

Caterpillars: The worst species are those that attack flowers, fruit and vegetables shortly before harvest. Caterpillars of swift moth and winter moth feed on roots and leaves respectively of a variety of host plants. Cabbage caterpillars attack brassicas all summer and sometimes hand picking is not enough.

Use derris (dust or spray), pyrethrum, or a preparation of *Bacillus thuringensis* which harms nothing but caterpillars.

Looper caterpillars appear mainly in autumn but rarely in large numbers. They are voracious foliage feeders, so pick them off quickly when holes are seen. They mostly feed under leaves and hide by stretching out along veins. Hand picking also copes with **tortrix** caterpillars which attack shrubs and pip fruits. They stick two leaves or a leaf onto a fruit, to hide.

Codling moths: burrow into apples and pears. Spraying becomes essential when other control measures prove inadequate,

CORRUGATED
CARDBOARD
GRUB TRAPS

Caterpillar damage to a cabbage leaf.

and water. Cover the jars with a 1/2 cm wire mesh or a plastic mesh fruit bag, to exclude larger insects. After an initial attack clean and reset the traps. After the grubs have fed they leave fruit and rapidly pupate, so that a further generation can appear in as little as five to six weeks, when they will need further spraying. A second or sometimes third generation overwinters.

but it must be carefully timed since grubs inside fruit will be immune.

The grubs overwinter in bark cracks and litter around trees, but many fall victim to birds and predatory insects like wasps and earwigs while looking for hiding places. Hens and other predators can give almost 100 per cent control of those in the soil.

Provide artificial pupating sites by tying rolls of corrugated cardboard around the main limbs of trees in summer. Inspect the trees regularly and destroy the hiding grubs until all the fruit has been picked. Always clear away fallen fruit.

Set traps in trees, and when males appear in them spray the tree with pyrethrum, repeating a week later to catch hatching larvae. For traps use jam jars filled with a 50/50 solution of molasses or black treacle

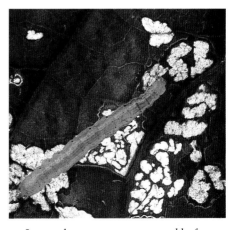

Looper damage to an ornamental leaf.

Tortrix caterpillars attack shrubs and pip fruit.

Carrots may be attacked by carrot rust fly.

A codling moth trap in a plastic fruit net.

Carrot Rust Fly: grubs tunnel into roots of carrots, parsnips and celery. Deflect low-flying adults by surrounding vegetable plots with barriers of clear plastic.

Aphids, Whitefly and Thrips: Aphids and whitefly suck sap, while thrips rasp leaves, turning them silver. Use pyrethrum, or preferably potassium soap preparations which do not harm other insects. Only adult whiteflies are vulnerable, so repeat spraying is necessary, or use bright yellow boards made sticky with motor oil. Remove aphids with a strong water jet.

Scales and Mealy Bugs: Scales live under protective hard wax coverings. Hand pick them off the plant or spray them with lime sulphur or spraying oil. Mealy bugs are well protected by soft wax scales; dab them with methylated spirits or smother them with oil.

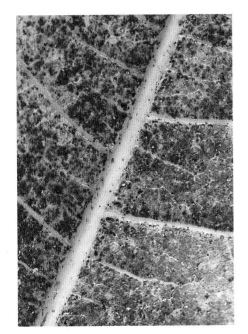

Leaf damage caused by thrips.   *White wax scale insects on a citrus stem.*

Birds are the natural predators of many insect pests.

Bunches of grapes can be bagged against wasps and birds.

Mites: are pinhead-sized suckers that feed under leaves, causing speckles and browning. A common glasshouse pest, they are active in dry air, and can be controlled by potassium soaps, sulphur preparations

Snails become active in warm, moist conditions.

and by smothering with spraying oil.

Miscellaneous: Birds and wasps often damage fruit. A wire cage or net deter birds, although individual fruits or bunches can be bagged against birds and wasps. Enclose the fruit in either white paper bags or old nylon stockings as it begins to colour fastened tightly around the stalk.

Slugs or snails: become active in warm, moist conditions, mainly at night when they can be collected in quantity during a torchlight tour of the garden. Many are eaten by birds. Snails become dormant when it is very dry, hot or cold and can be found hiding in sheltered corners or in thicket plants like flax and pampas.

Shallow saucers of stale beer set on the ground will trap slugs. Barriers of loose sand, sawdust or ashes will deter slugs and snails by reducing their traction.

Pears are susceptible to fireblight infection.

DISEASES

Viruses: cause pale or brown marks to appear on leaves, breaks in flower colour, distortion and death. They spread mainly through insects and hands. Infected plants cannot be cured, they must be destroyed.

Leaf spot: is caused by numerous fungi or bacteria, over wintered on debris. Good garden hygiene and balanced feeding are preventive measures. They can be controlled with copper sprays.

Fireblight: a notifiable disease, is serious on pip fruits, especially pears. The shoots shrivel up and the leaves become brown and hang down. Cut back into clean tissue and disinfect your hands and tools.

Fungi: cause the majority of diseases.

Powdery mildews: are a white powder coat of spores on leaves, shoots and fruit at their worst in dry weather, or in humid poorly ventilated greenhouses. Some are specific to host plants while others attack a wide range of plants. Control by spraying with sulphur or baking soda if caught early. Prune and incinerate all infected shoot tips where the fungus overwinters.

Downy mildews: grow inside leaves and stems, eventually killing them, releasing spores in to the soil. Tissues commonly become soft and brown, with a white fuzz of fungus beneath, but rose leaves turn purple. Spray plants with copper to protect them. Potato/tomato blight is related to this mildew. In potatoes, many blighted tubers can be avoided if the haulm is removed before digging. A common source of infection are potatoes accidentally left in the ground at harvest time.

Rusts: have a complex life cycle, attacks underside of leaves in summer to cause

Onions are often affected by downy mildews.

Weeping willow rust.

premature leaf fall, then spreads rapidly by orange or brown spores lead to systemically attack the total plant. Potassium deficient plants are most prone to rust infection, including broad beans, raspberries, chives, roses, antirrhinums and hollyhocks. Cut and burn diseased shoots and growth, with autumn debris to eliminate the over wintering stage of spores. Copper sprays protect clean foliage.

In roses, orange summer spores spread rapidly to new foliage, until falling leaves in autumn carry a brown-spore rest stage. If rust develops on just a few new spring growth leaves, their removal may stop all further infection.

Celery spot: is usually caused by infected seed. If noticed early it can be controlled by hand picking and several sprayings with

copper. Feed established plants with a compost containing potash to avoid soft growth of the plant.

All sorts of fungi cause leaf spots, many of which can be ignored, but if infestation is severe protect clean foliage with either sulphur or copper, either of which can also be applied to the wood in winter as a clean-up spray.

Black spot: mainly attacks heavily pruned roses such as hybrid teas, or climbers that have been lightly pruned. It over winters on leaves which should be burnt. It can also attack leaves and fruit of apples and pears. Apply copper foliar feed after pruning and after blossoming.

Clubroot: in cruciferous plants is caused by a slime mould, a soil dweller which attacks stocks, wallflowers, turnips, radishes and especially serious on *brassicas*. The disease is prevalent on acid, badly drained soil, so drainage improvement helps to prevent the trouble. It is very hard to control because of its long survival in the soil, but it can be suppressed by heavy liming and sometimes by a piece of rhubarb in the planting hole.

NOTE:

Sulphur products include dust, colloidal sulphur and lime sulphur.
Copper sprays are sold as Bordeaux mixture, and copper hydroxide or oxychloride.
Baking soda sprays can be prepared by dissolving 1 teaspoon in 1 litre of water.

INDEX

The page numbers in **bold** type indicate illustrations .